This Book belongs to:

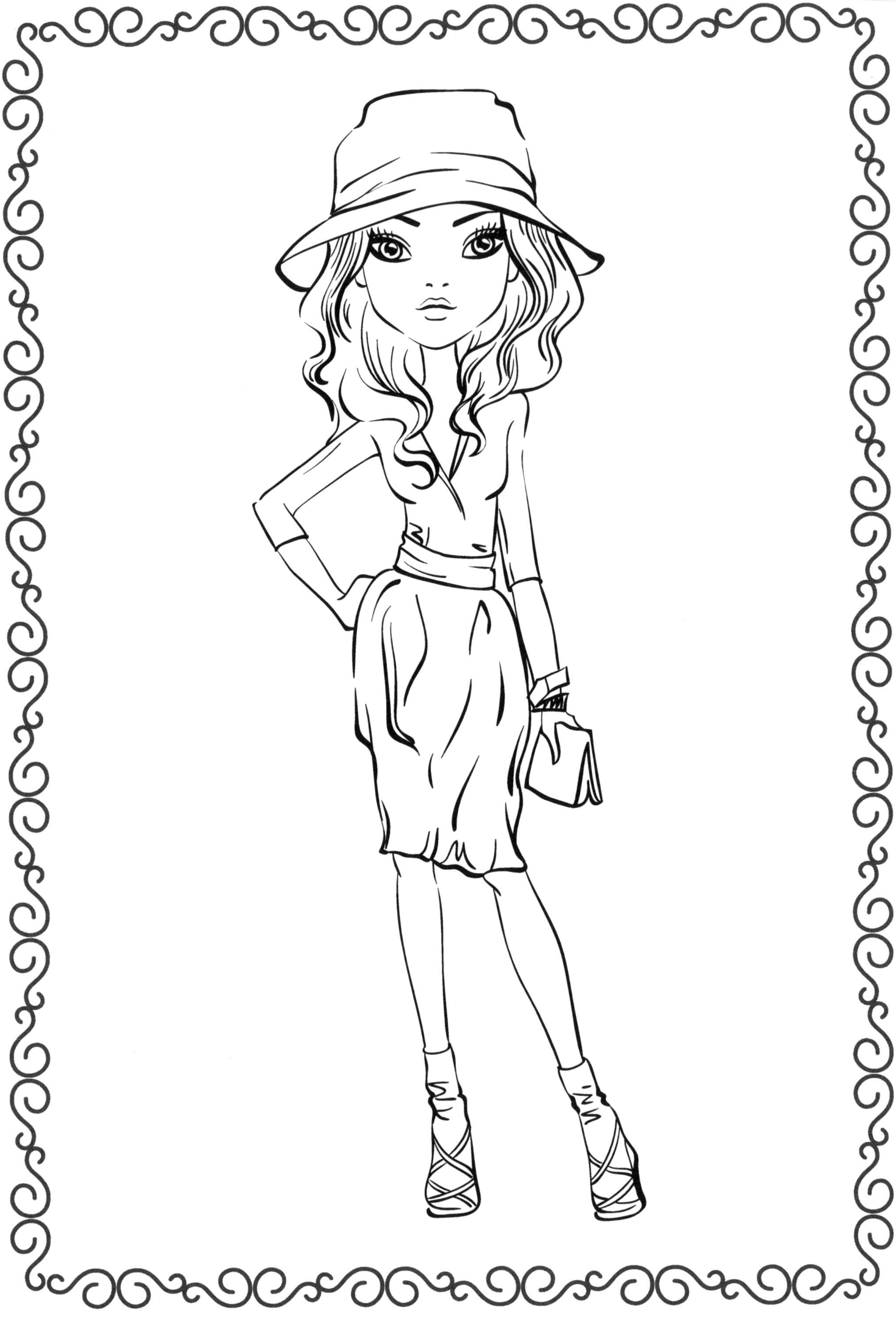

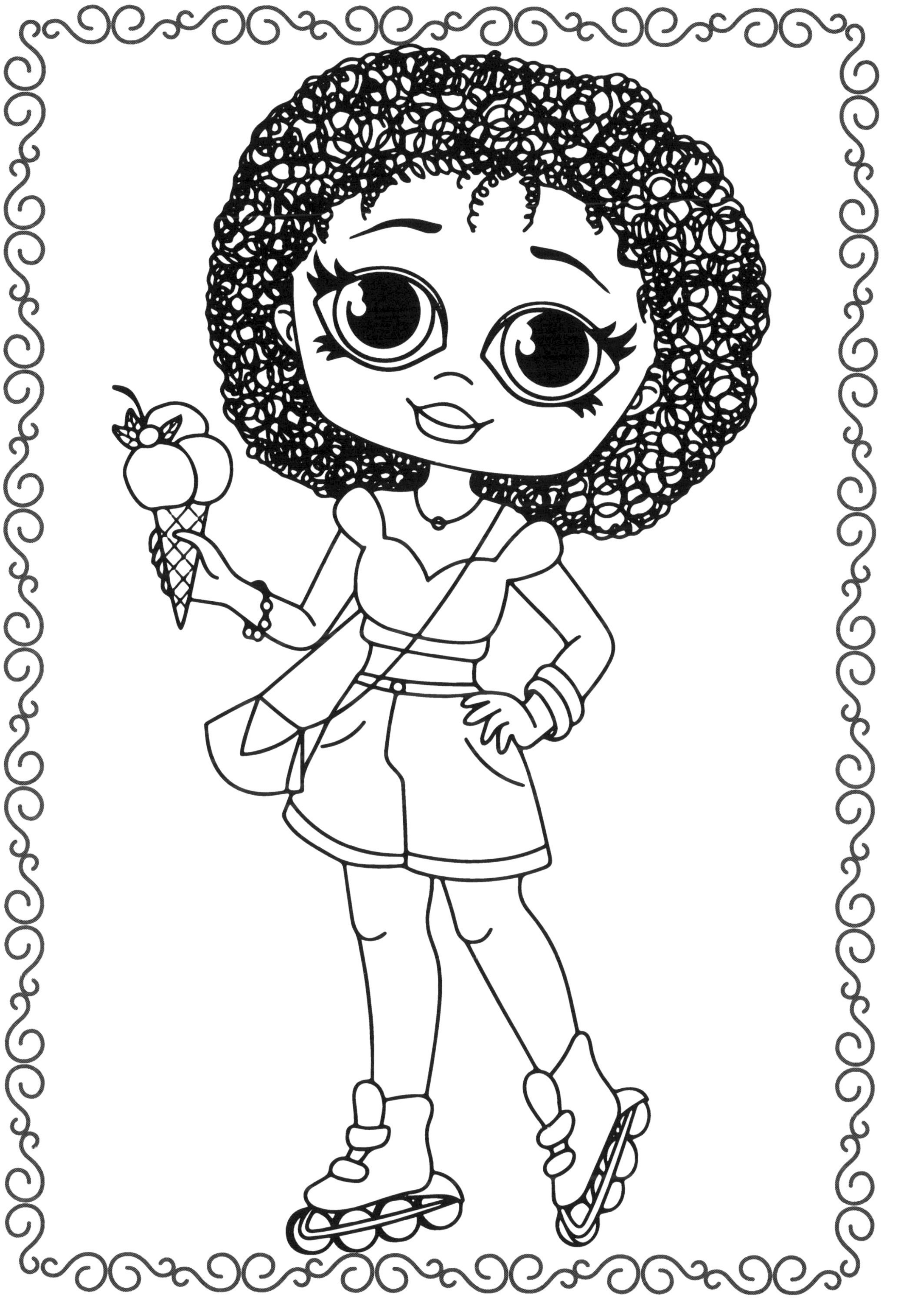

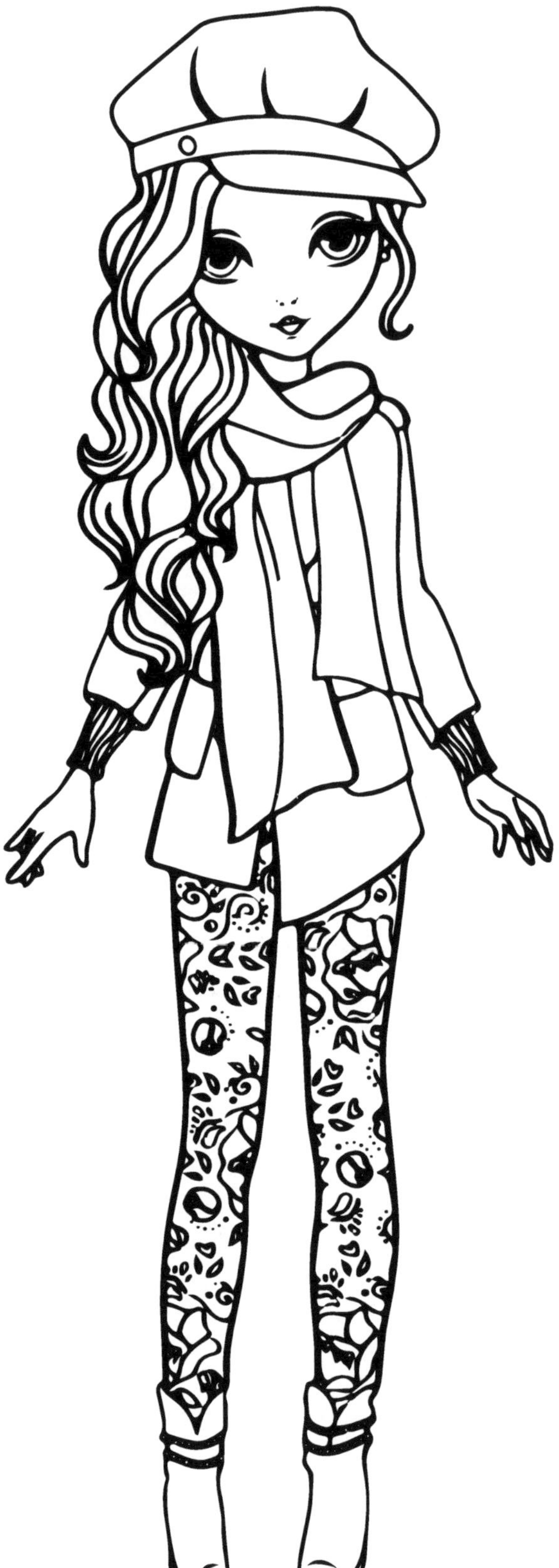

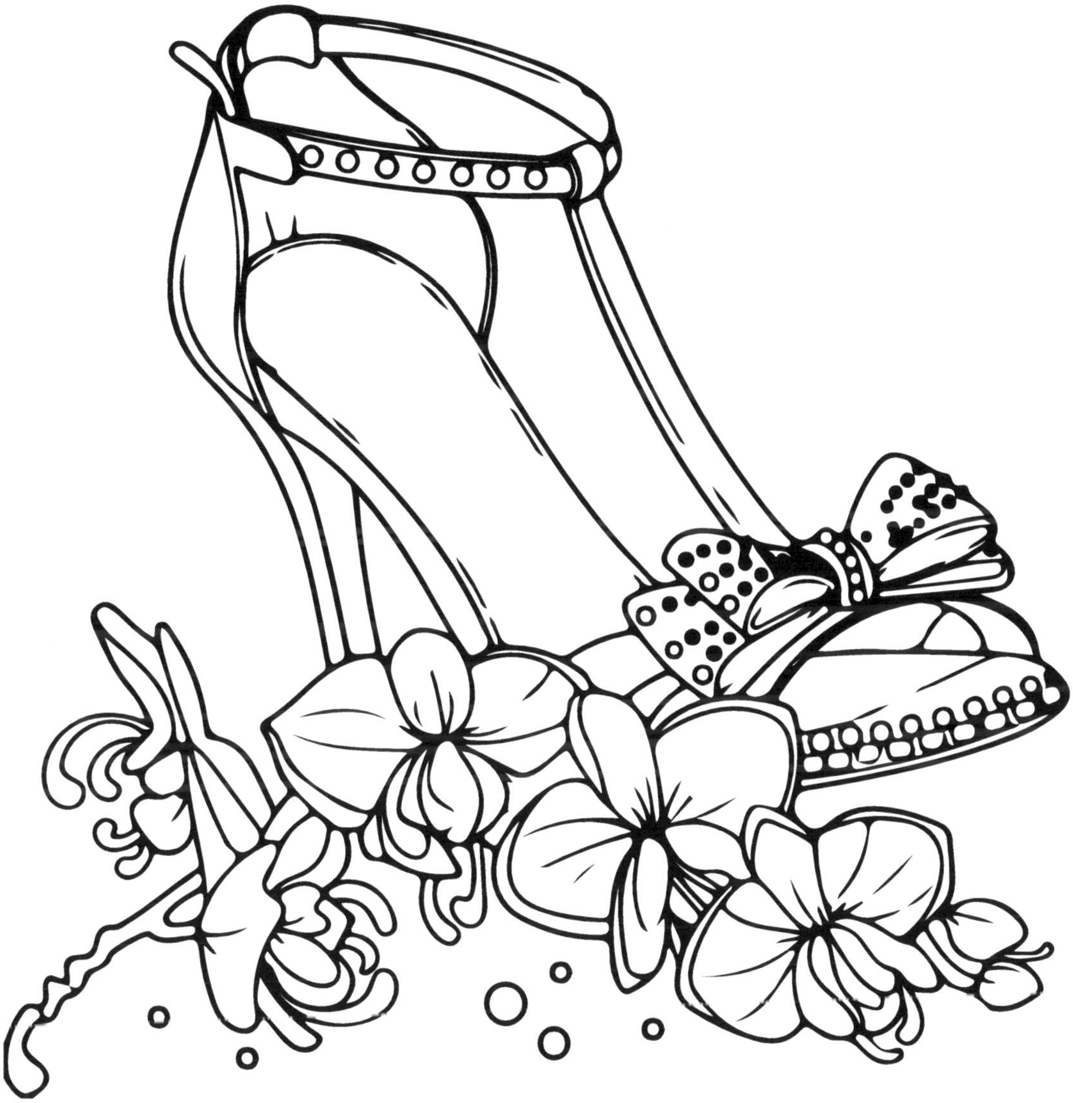

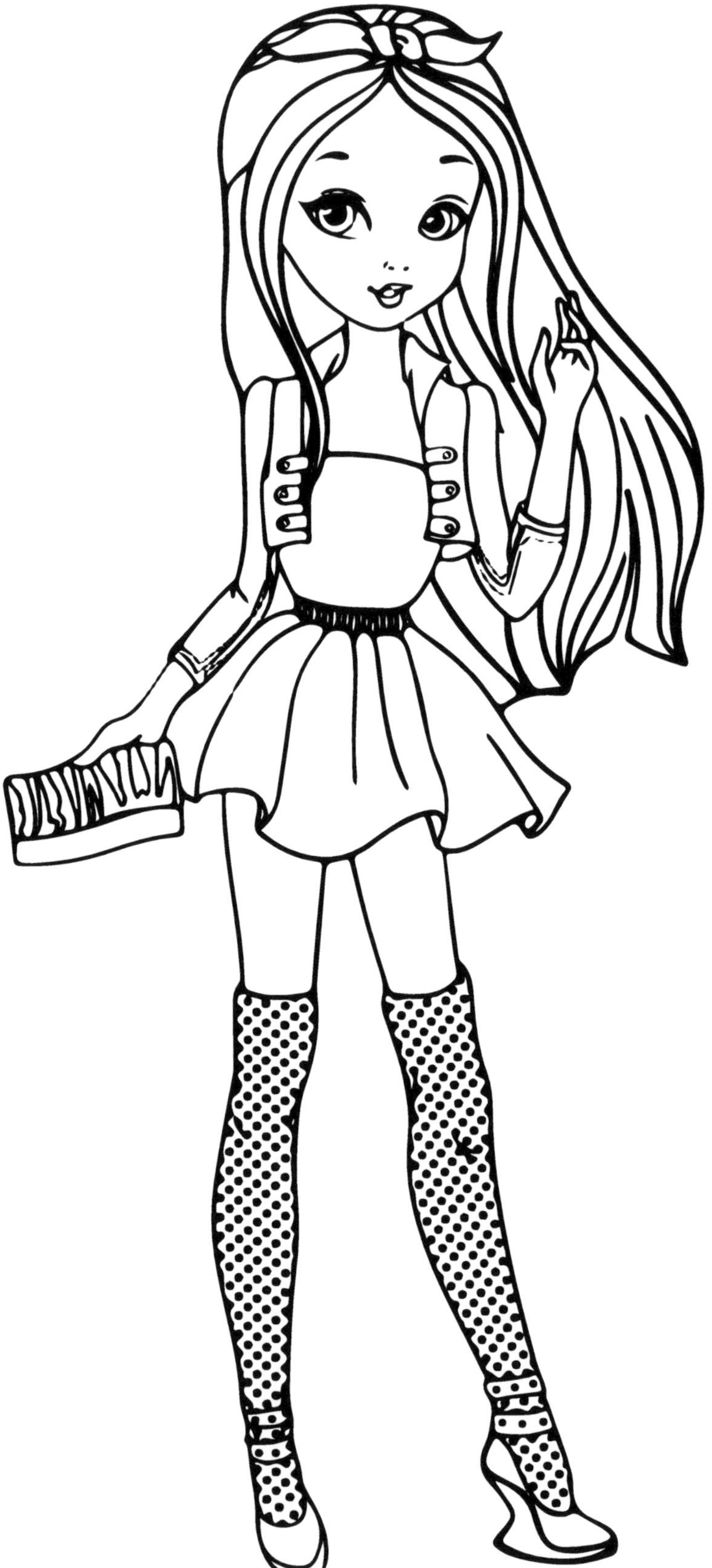

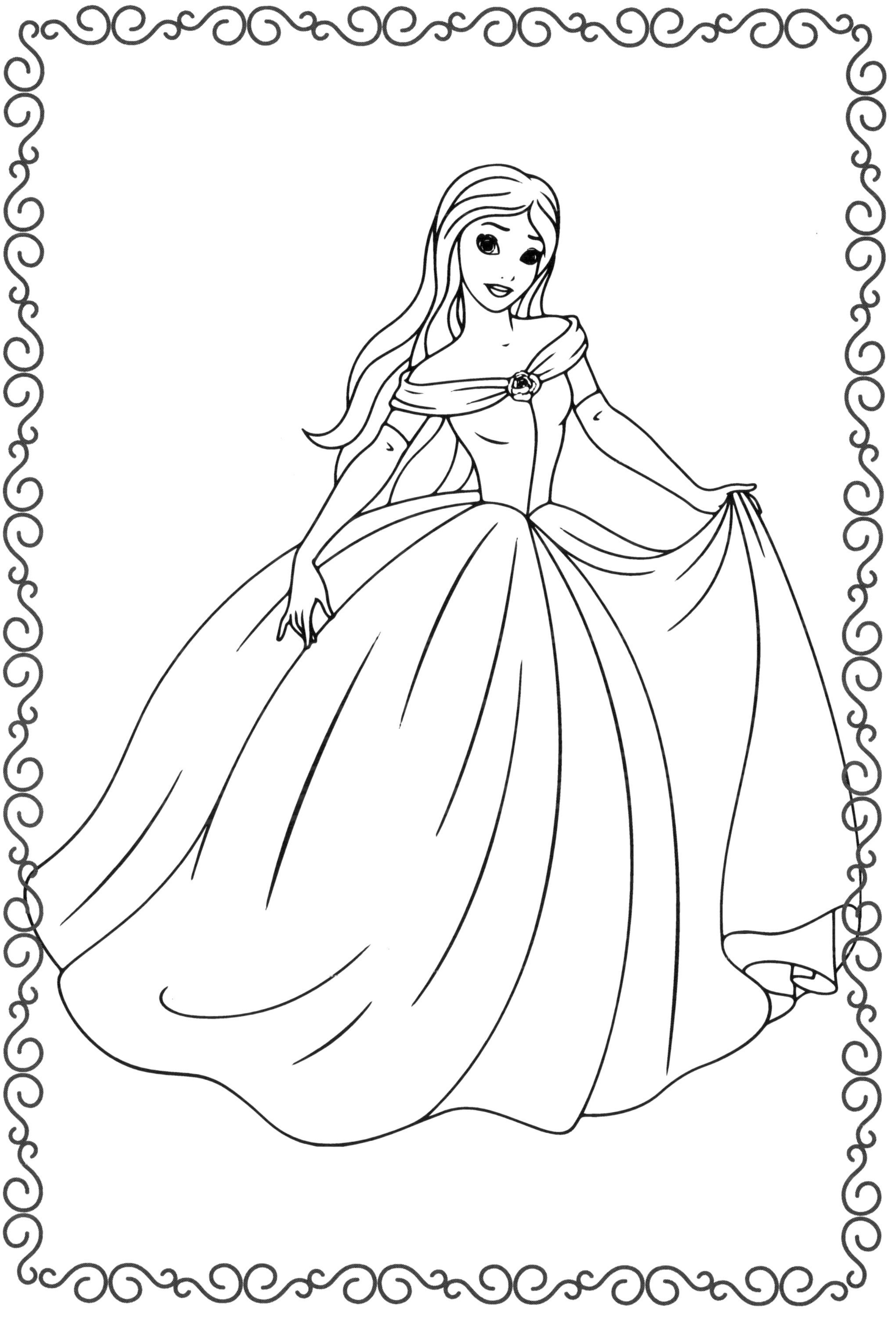

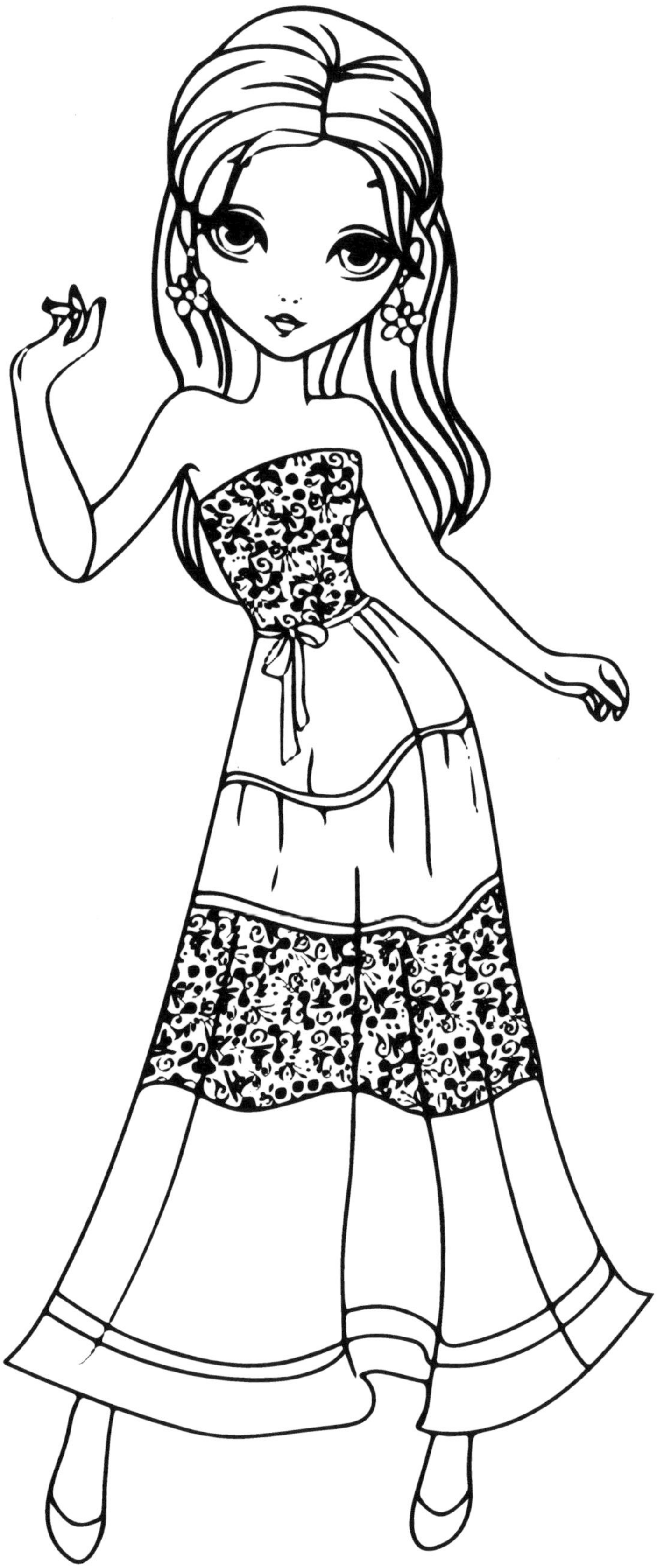

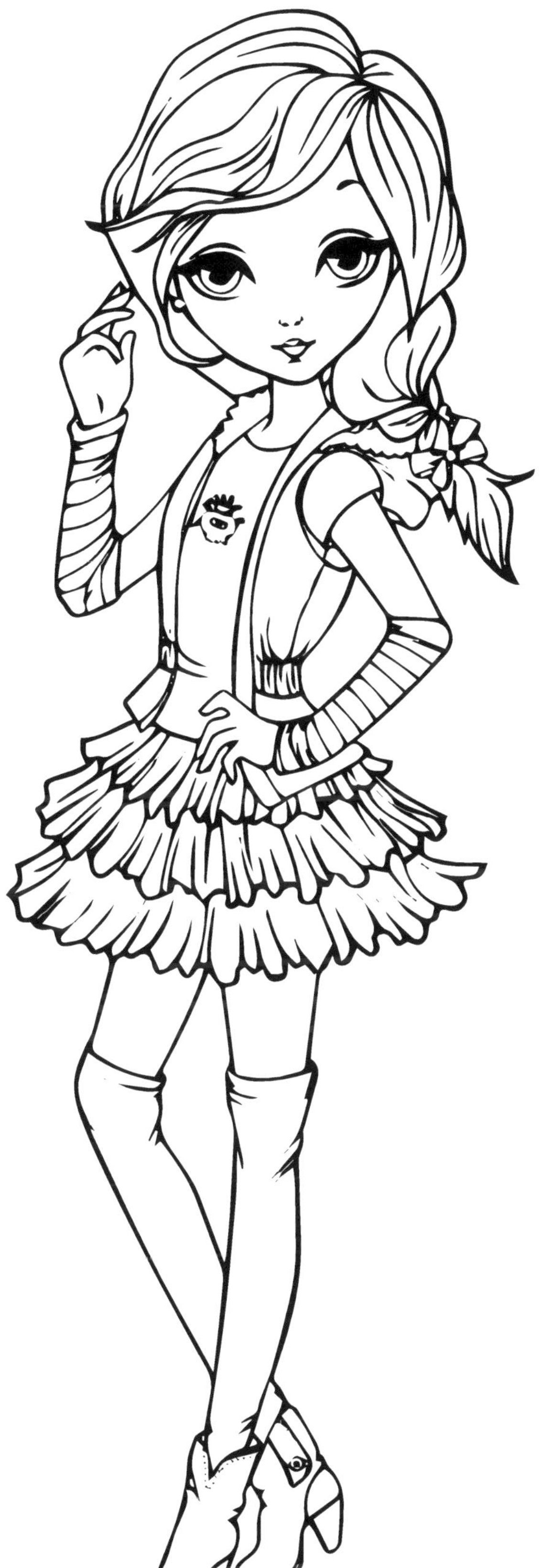

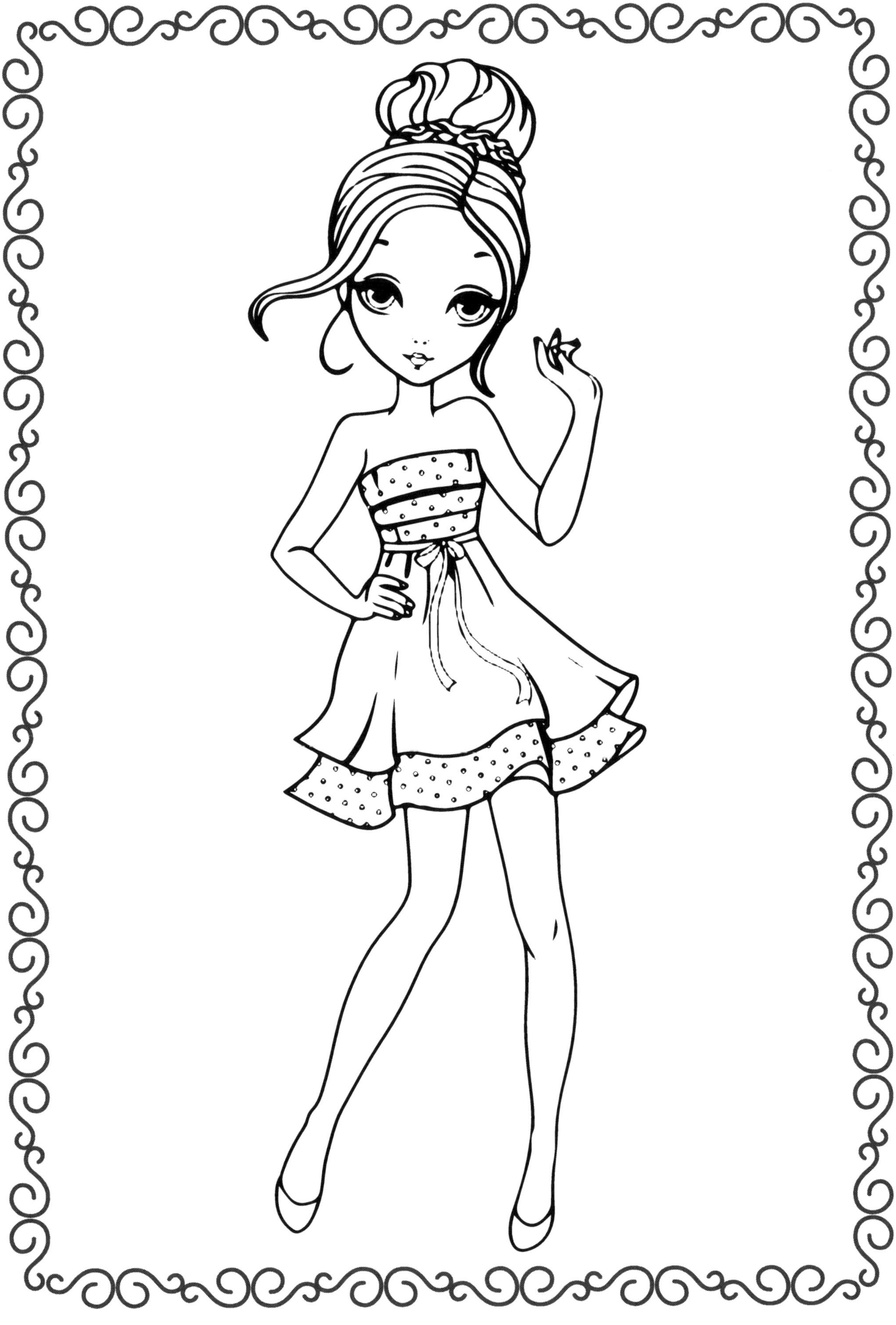

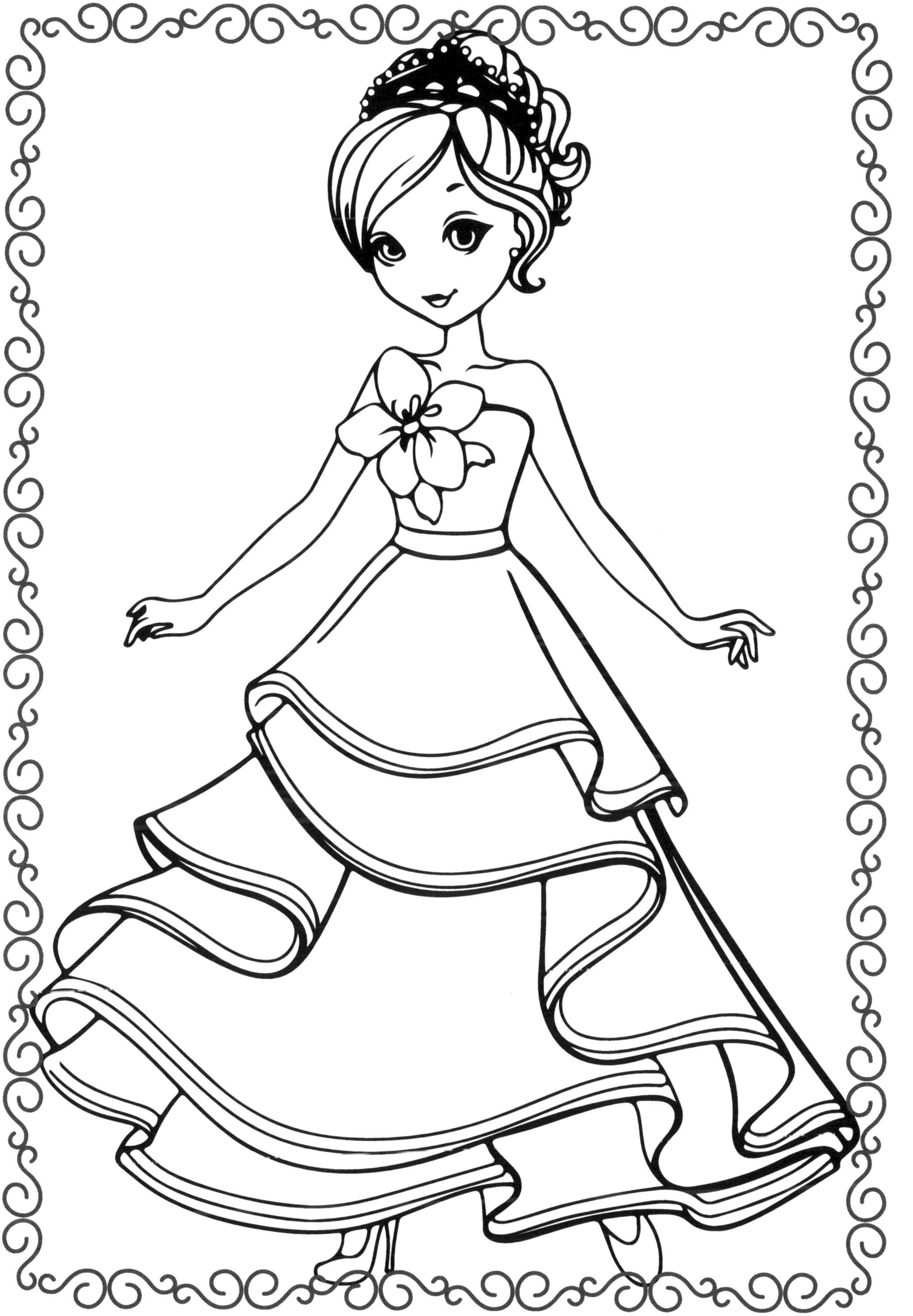

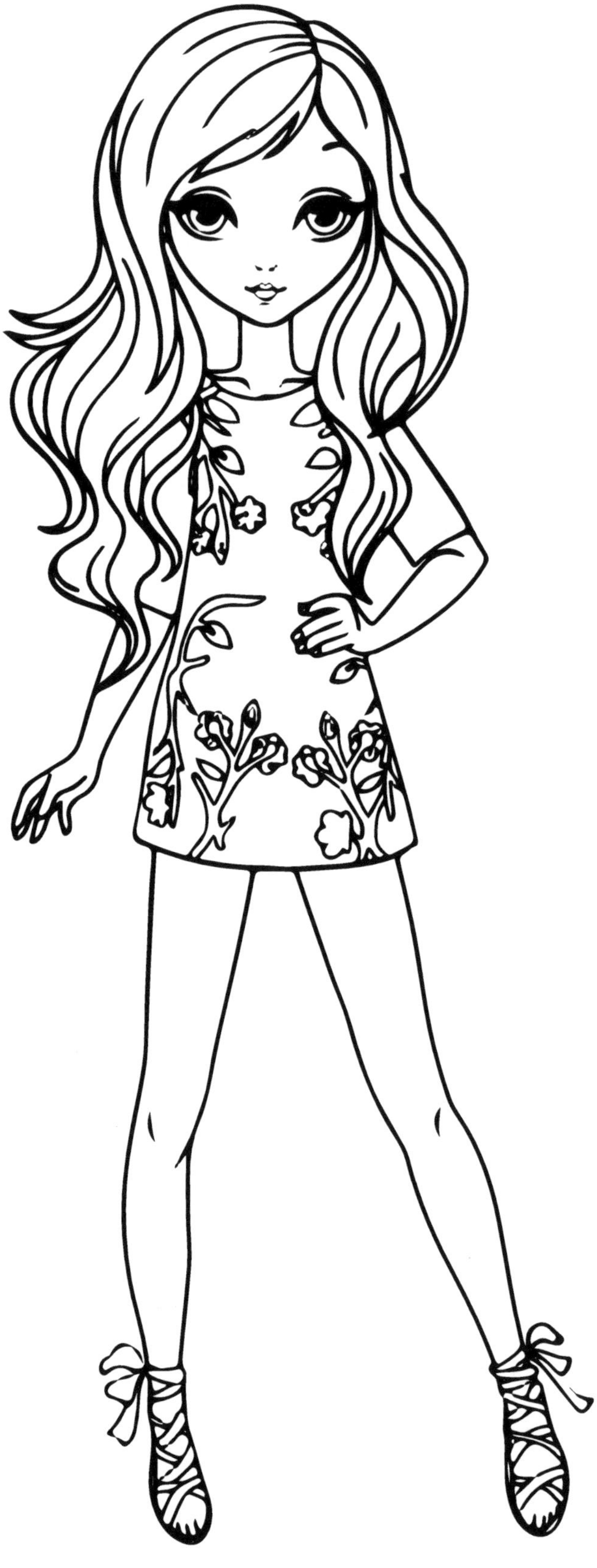

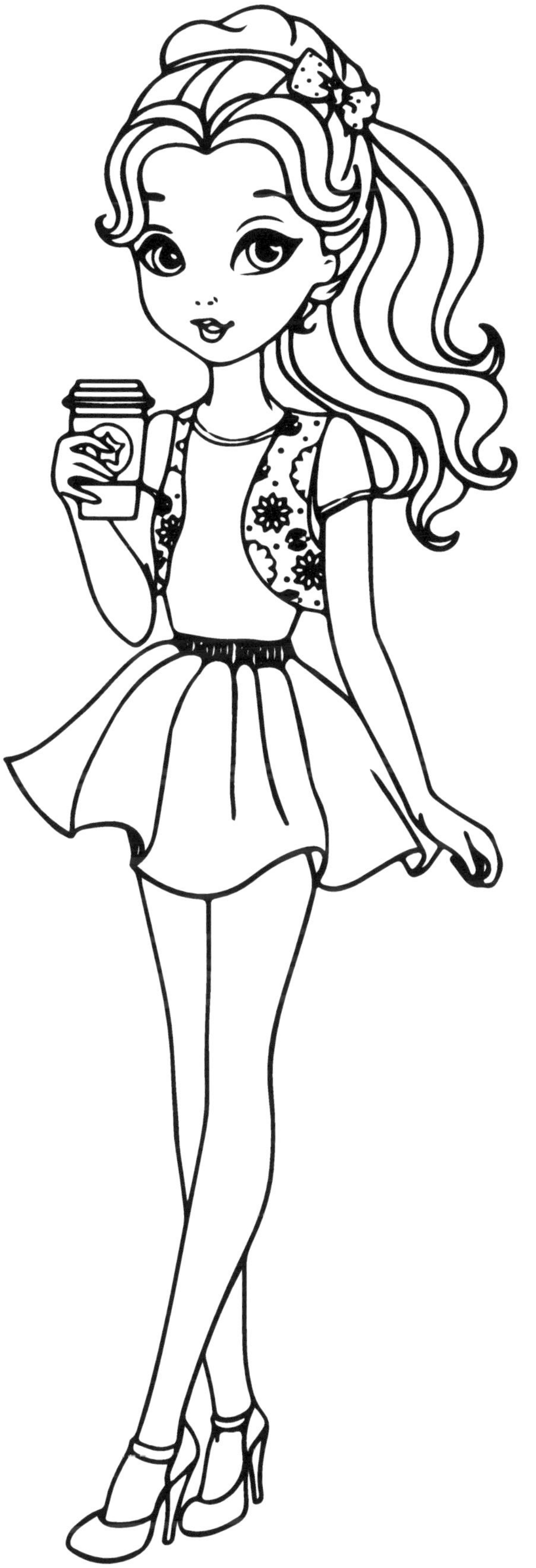

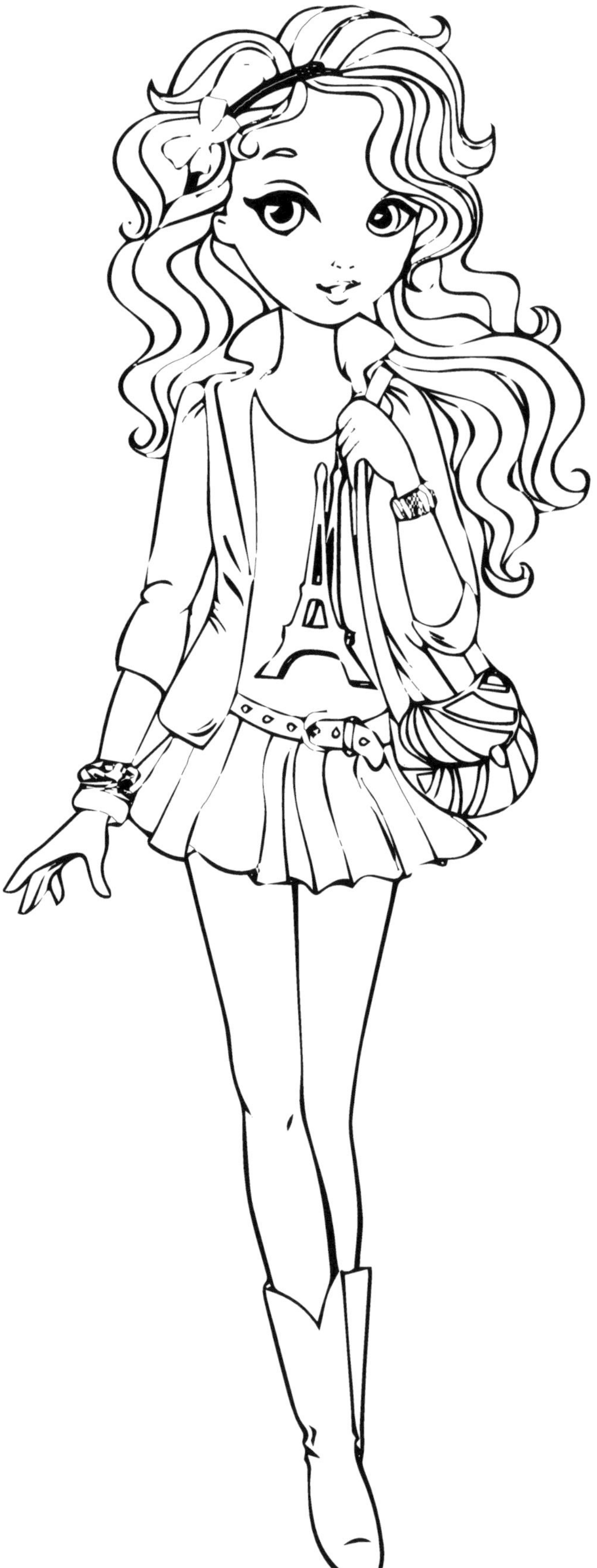

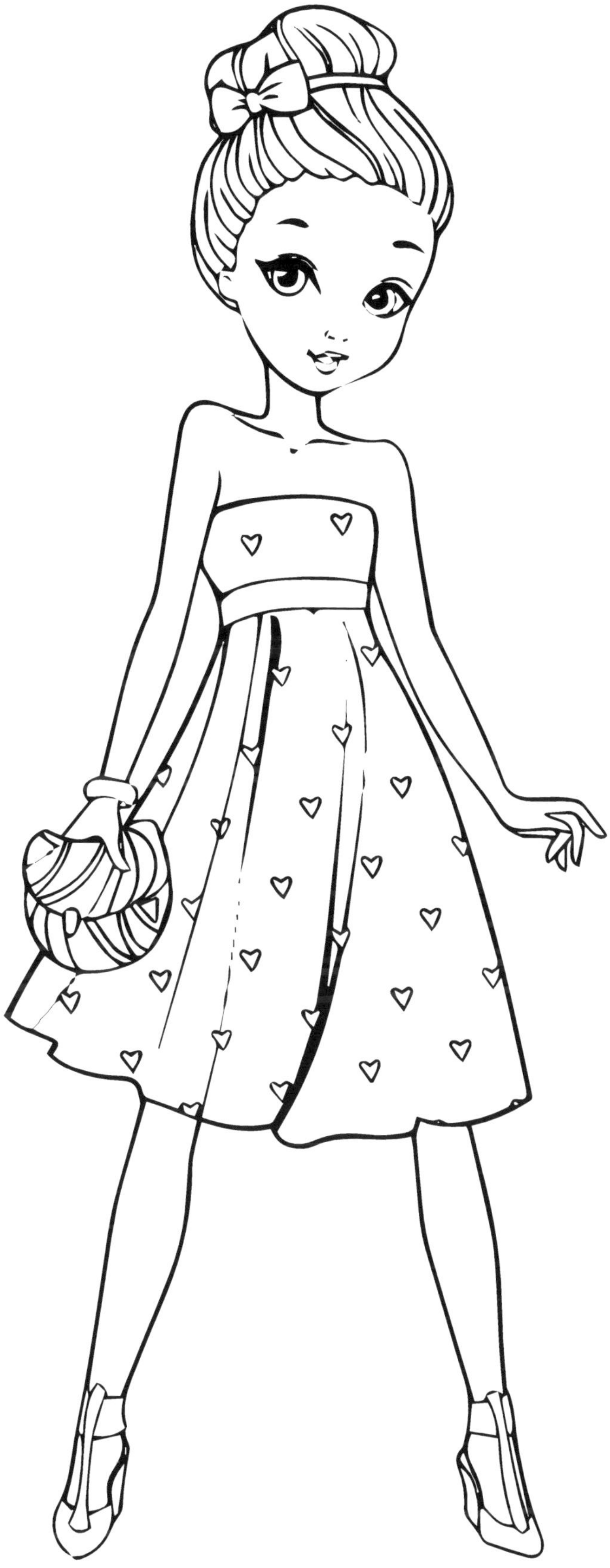

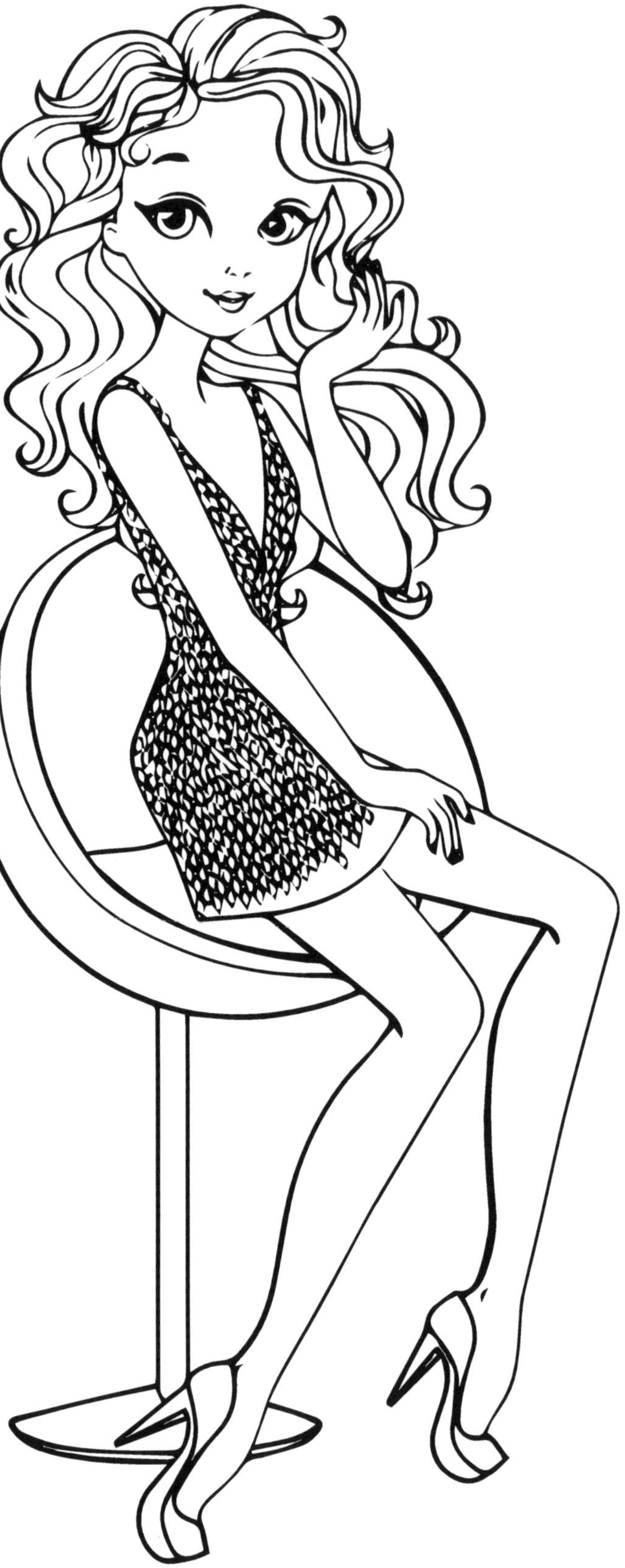

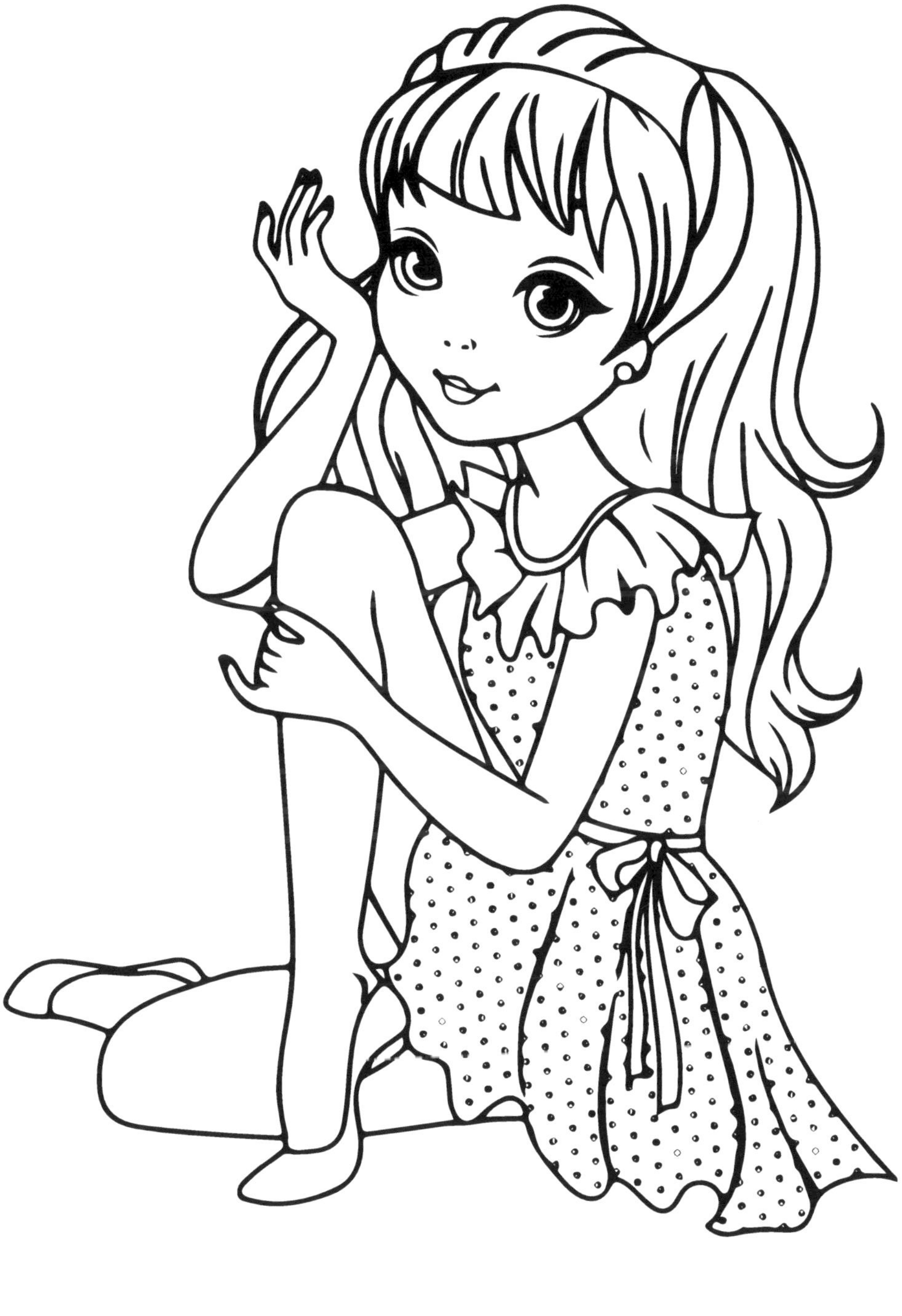

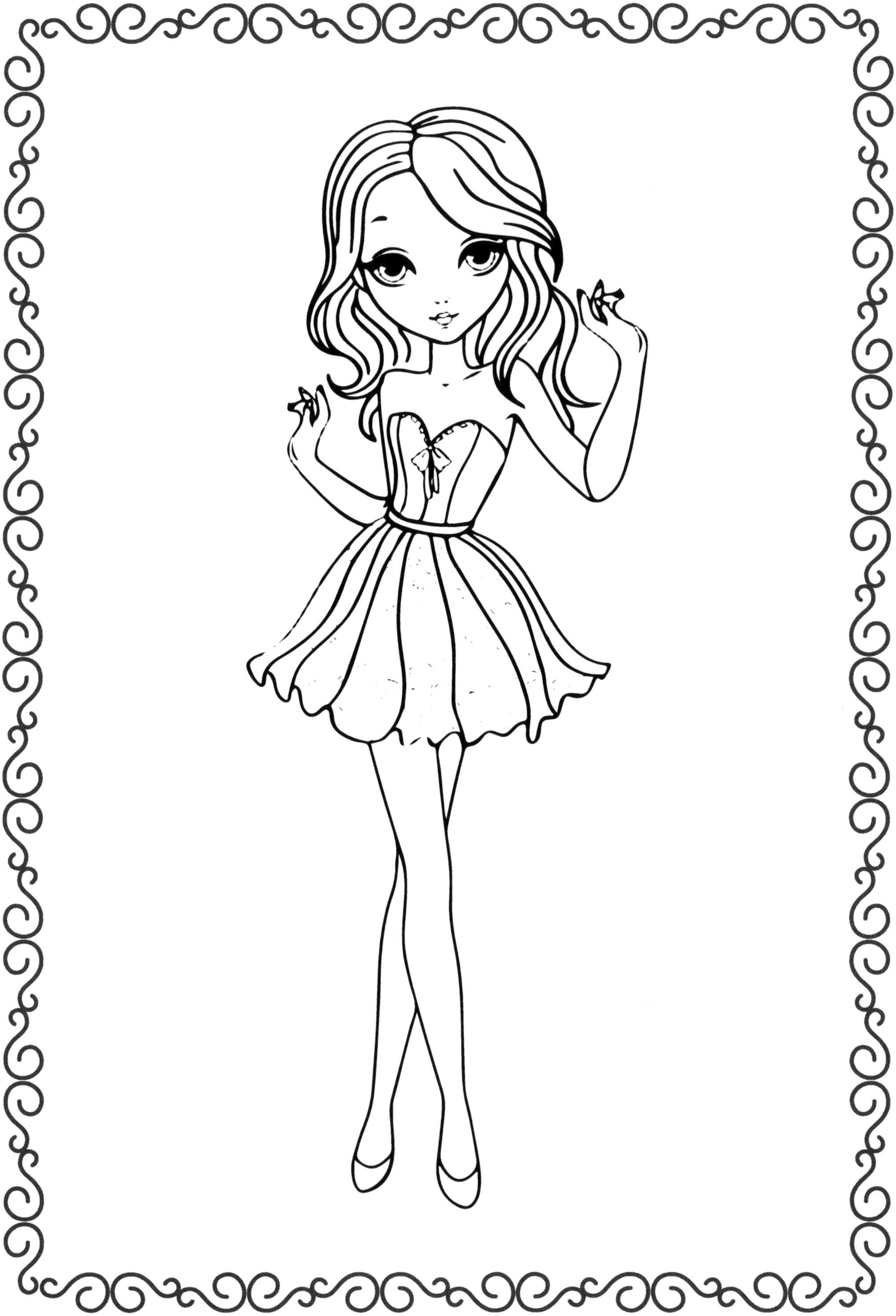

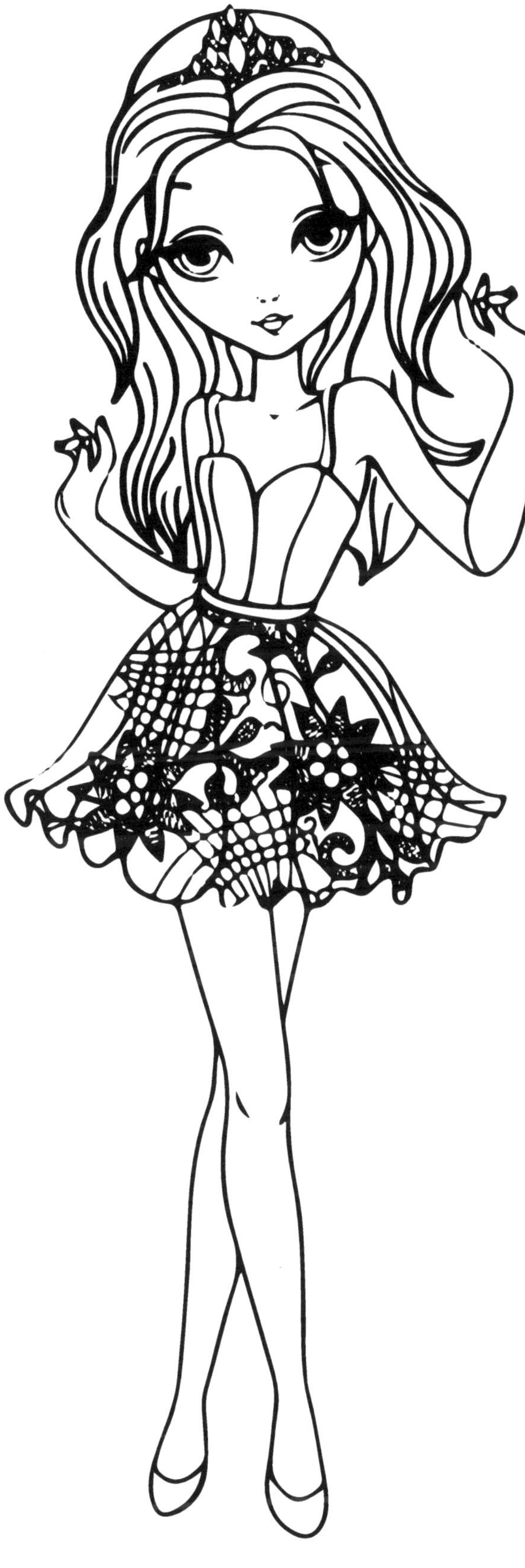

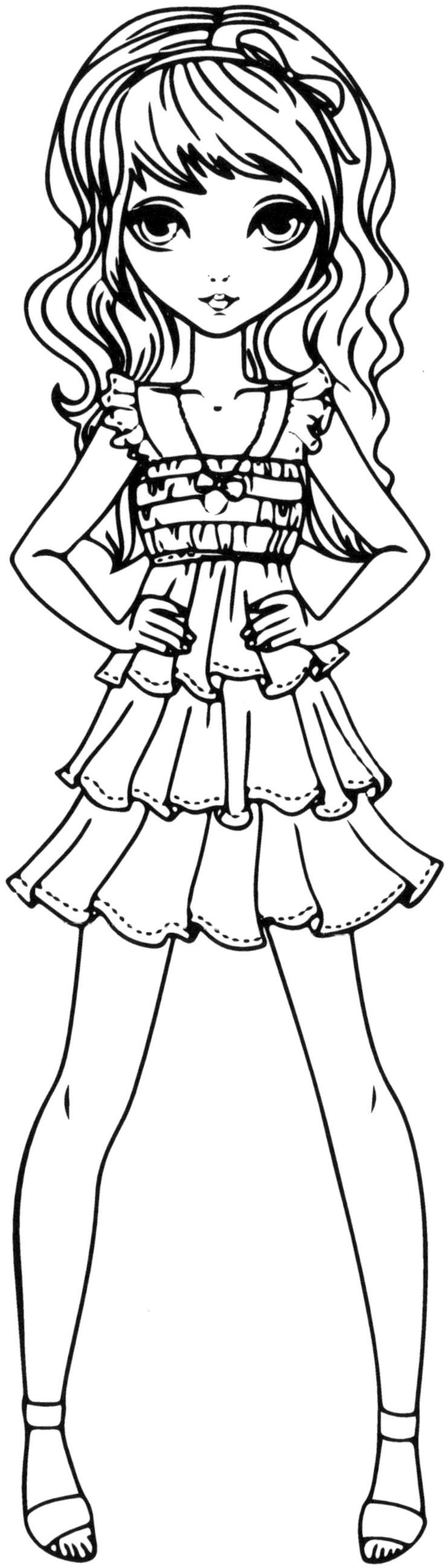

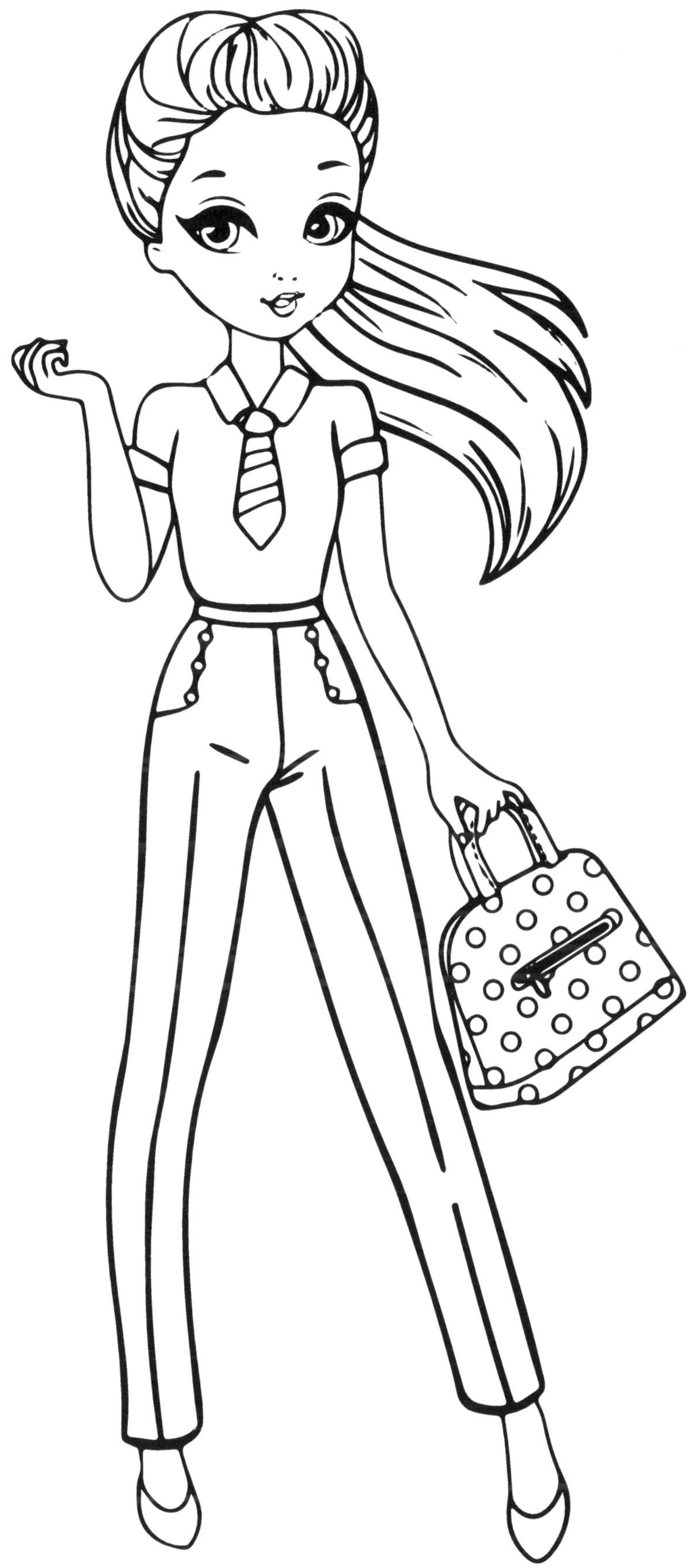

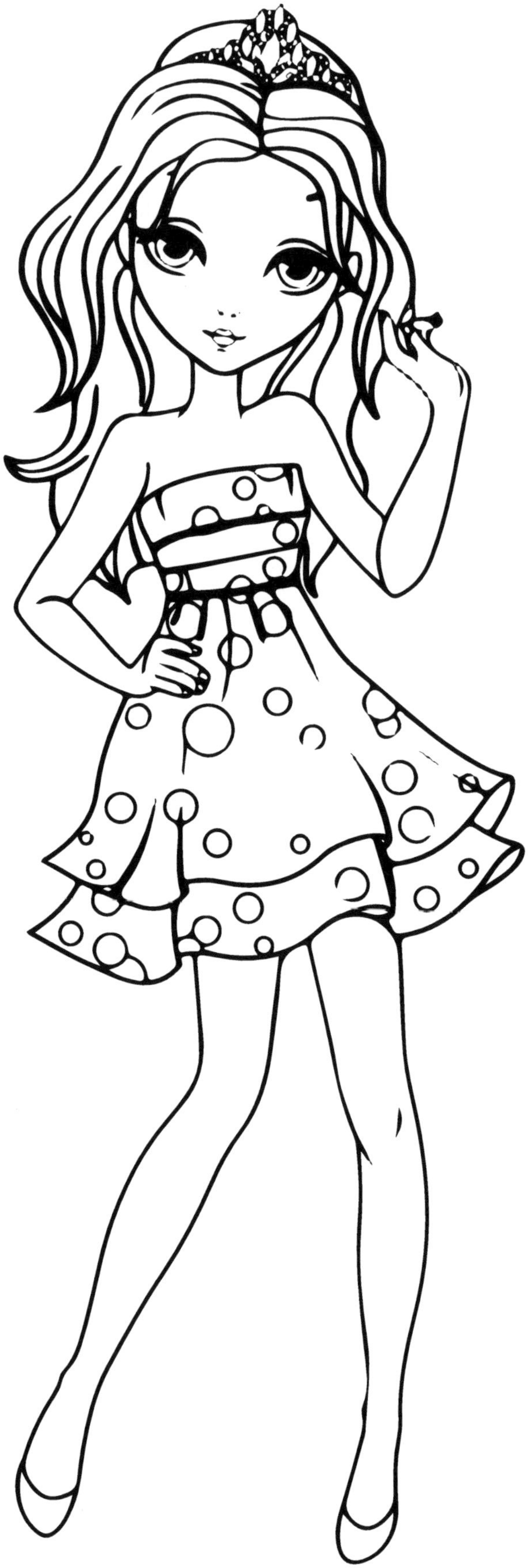

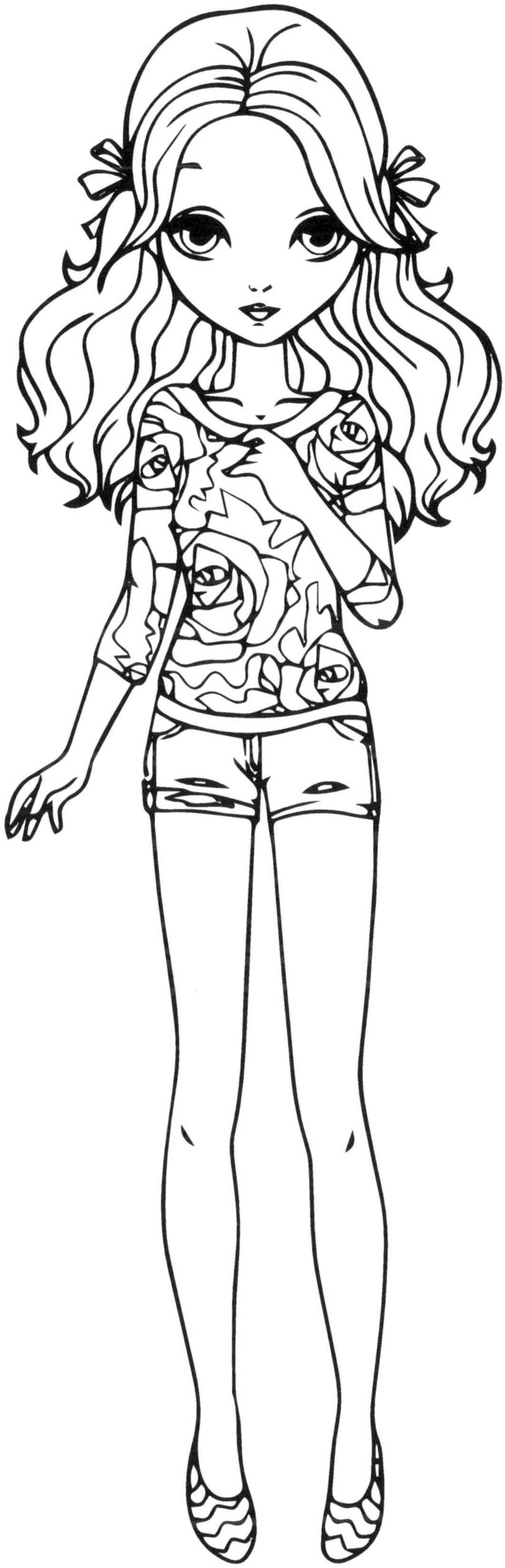

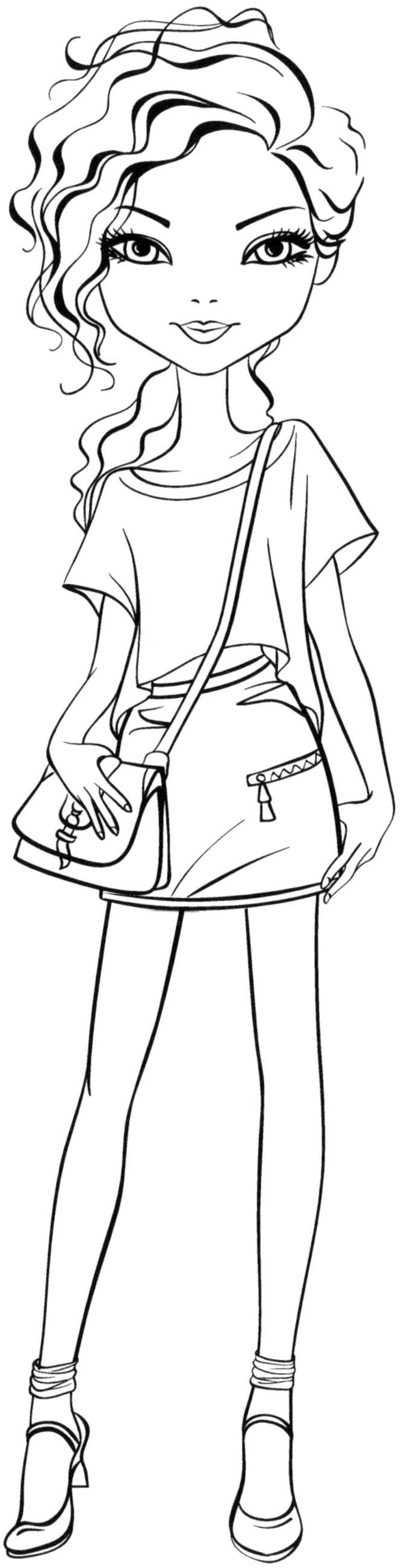

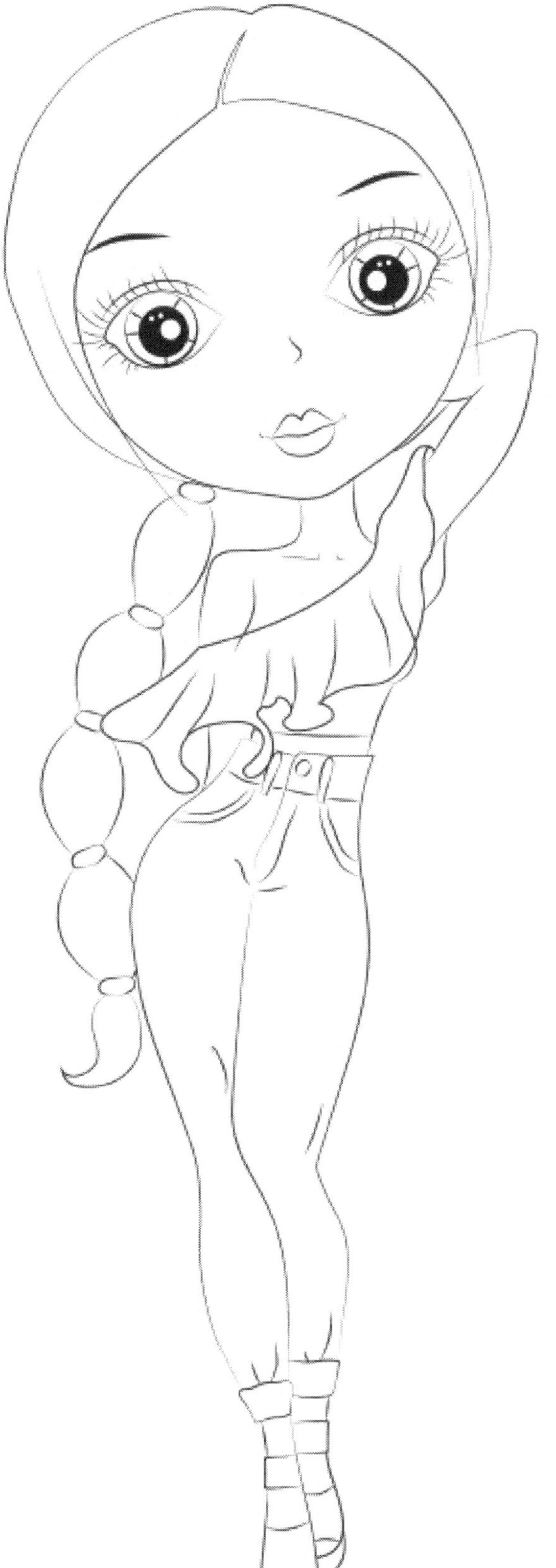

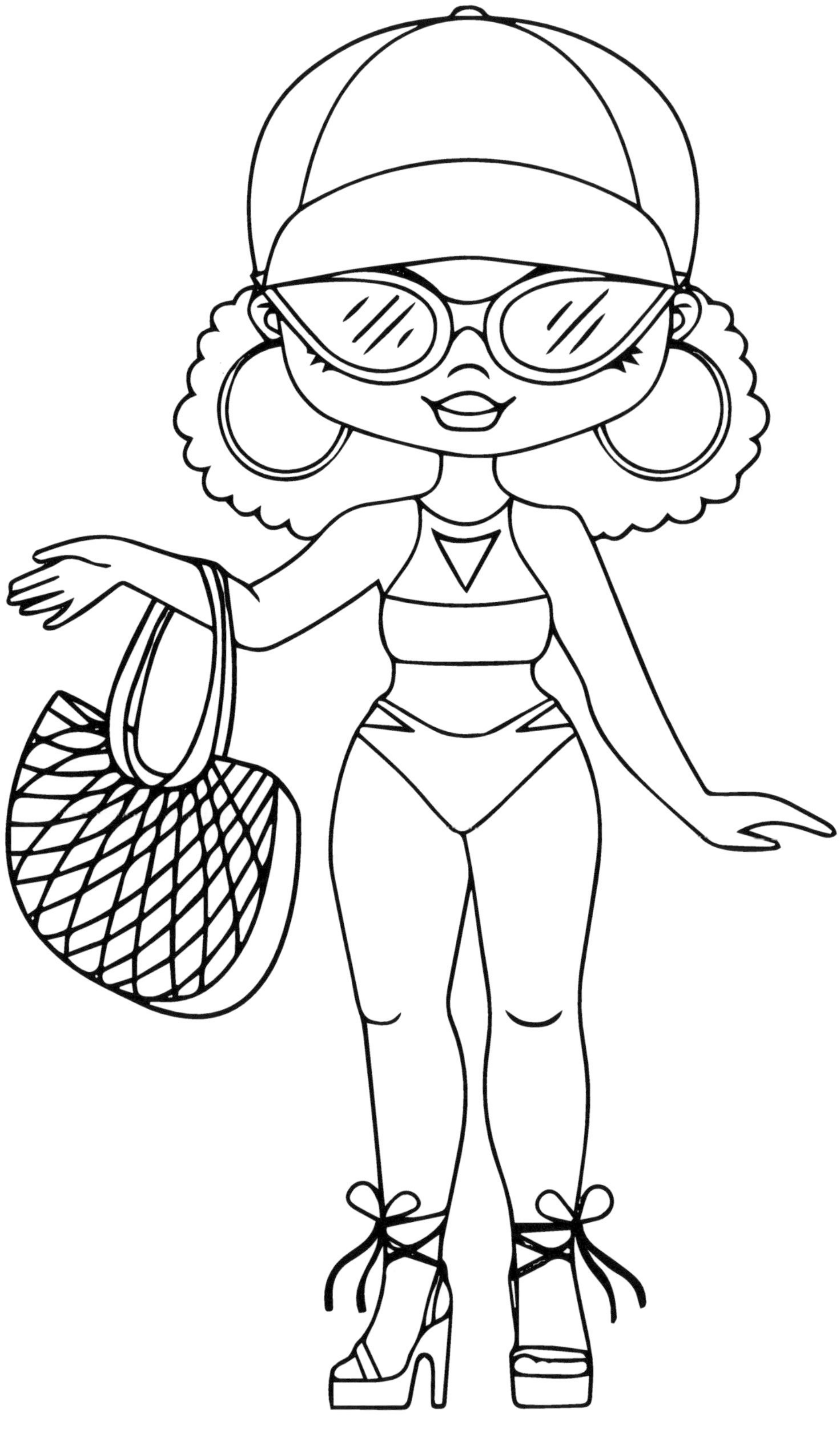

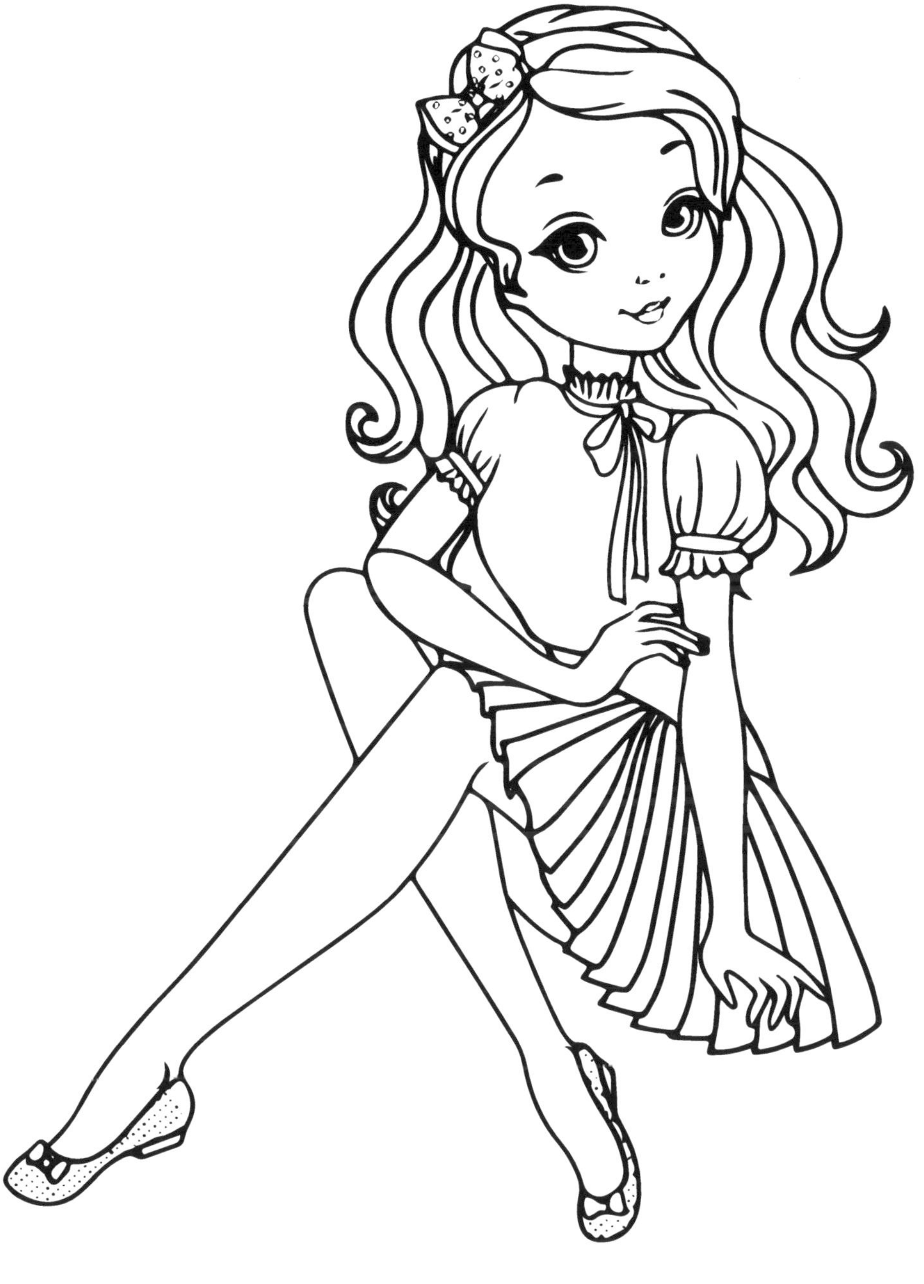

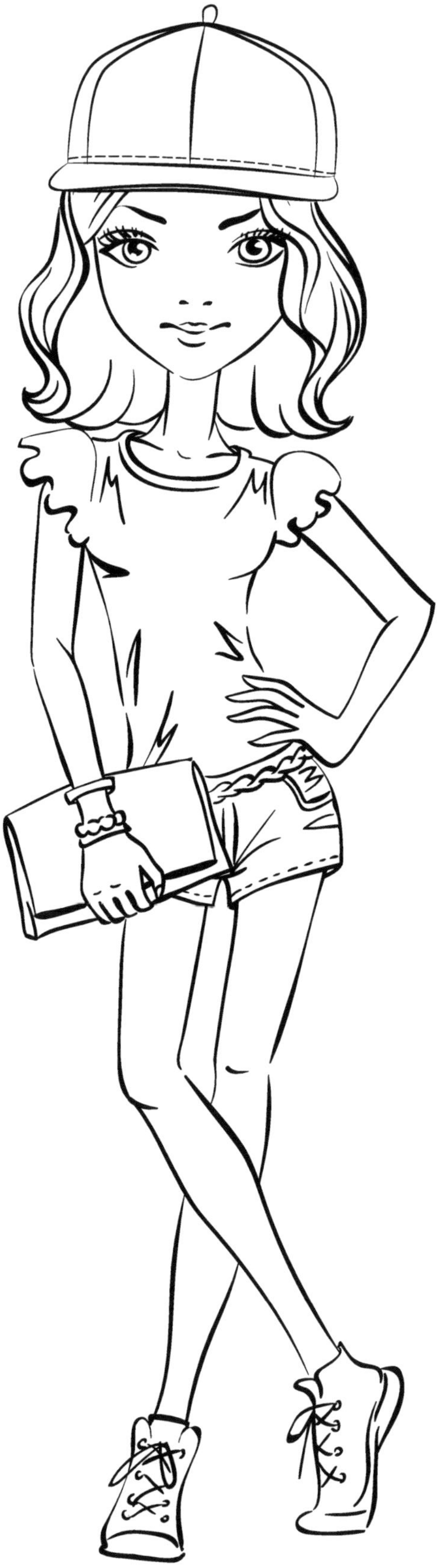

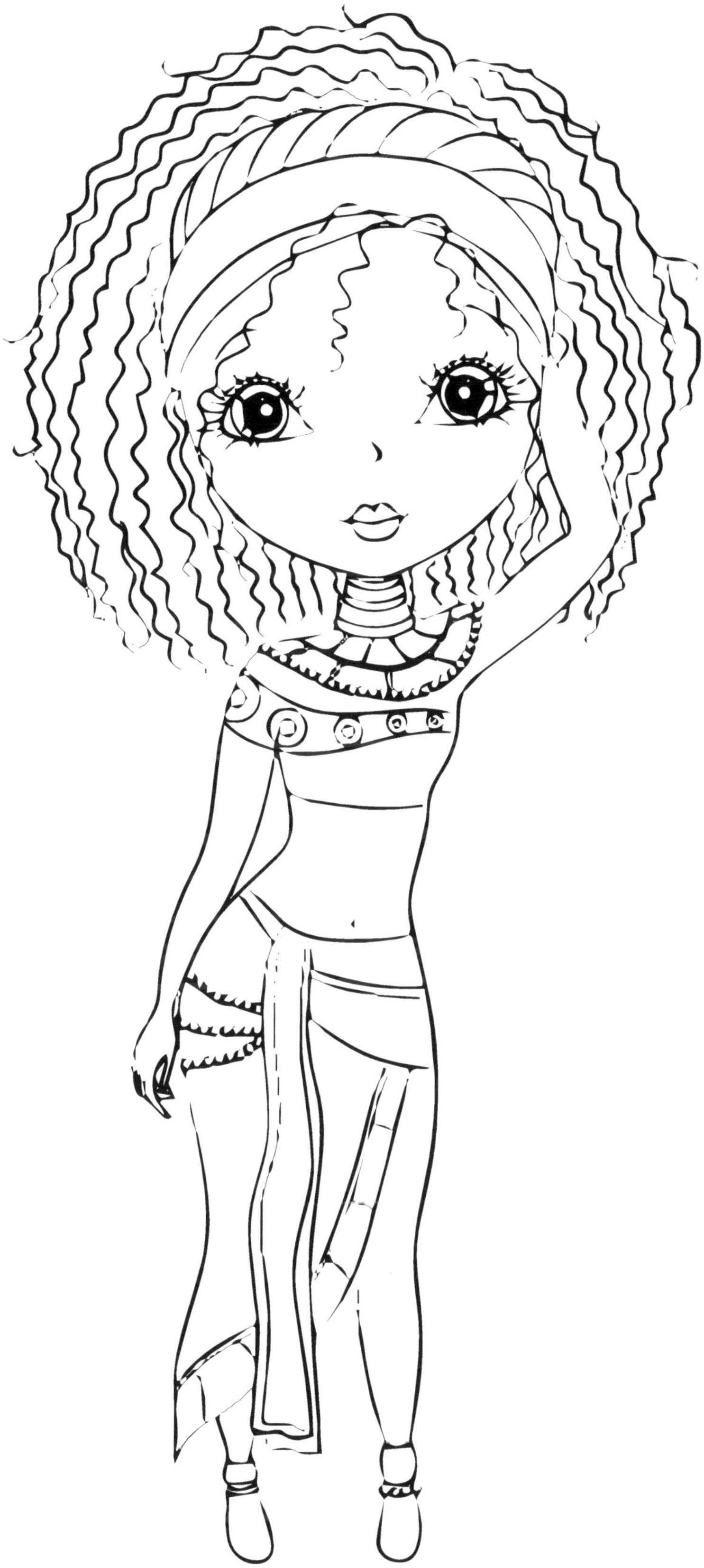

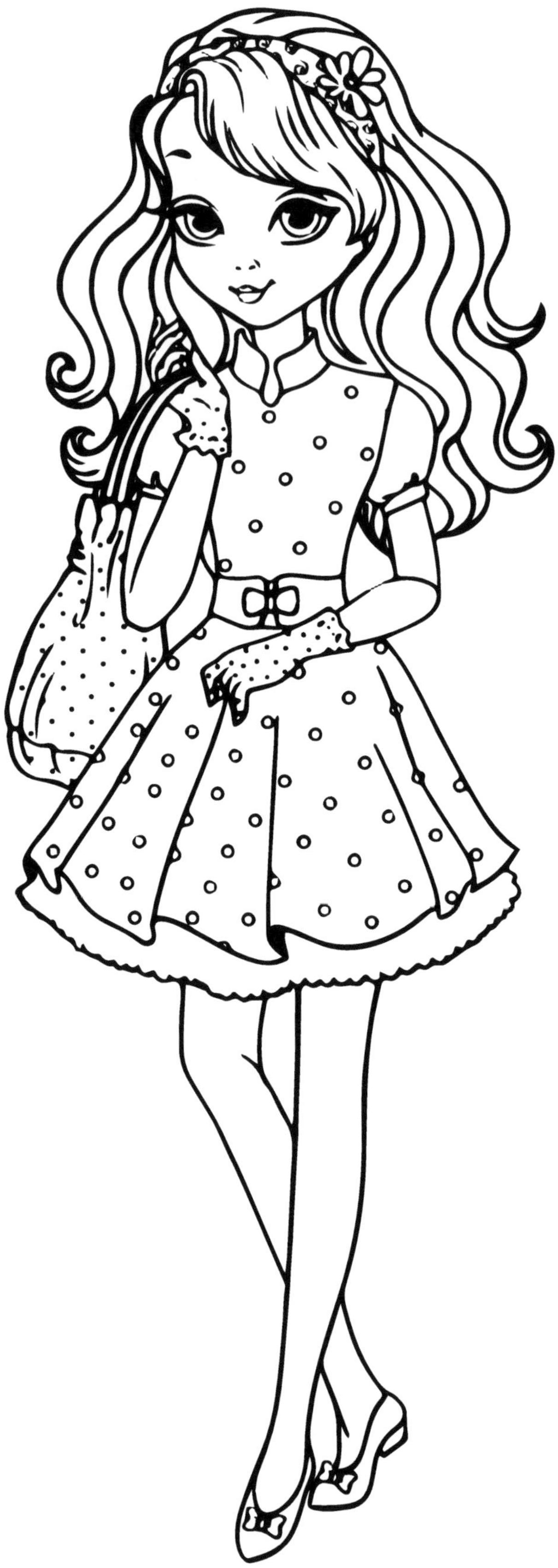

Printed in Great Britain
by Amazon

70861228R00018